IF F

Greater Than a Tourist Book Series
Reviews from Readers

I think the series is wonderful and beneficial for tourists to get information before visiting the city.

-Seckin Zumbul, Izmir Turkey

I am a world traveler who has read many trip guides but this one really made a difference for me. I would call it a heartfelt creation of a local guide expert instead of just a guide.

-Susy, Isla Holbox, Mexico

New to the area like me, this is a must have!

 -Joe, Bloomington, USA

This is a good series that gets down to it when looking for things to do at your destination without having to read a novel for just a few ideas.

-Rachel, Monterey, USA

Good information to have to plan my trip to this destination.

-Pennie Farrell, Mexico

Great ideas for a port day.

-Mary Martin USA

Aptly titled, you won't just be a tourist after reading this book. You'll be greater than a tourist!

-Alan Warner, Grand Rapids, USA

Even though I only have three days to spend in San Miguel in an upcoming visit, I will use the author's suggestions to guide some of my time there. An easy read - with chapters named to guide me in directions I want to go.

 -Robert Catapano, USA

Great insights from a local perspective! Useful information and a very good value!

 -Sarah, USA

This series provides an in-depth experience through the eyes of a local. Reading these series will help you to travel the city in with confidence and it'll make your journey a unique one.

-Andrew Teoh, Ipoh, Malaysia

>TOURIST

GREATER THAN A TOURIST- BITOLA MACEDONIA

(TRAVEL GUIDE BOOK FROM A LOCAL)

50 Travel Tips from a Local

Aleksandar Tashkovski

Greater Than a Tourist- Bitola Macedonia Copyright © 2019 by CZYK Publishing LLC. All Rights Reserved.

All rights reserved. No part of this book may be reproduced in any form or by any electronic or mechanical means including information storage and retrieval systems, without permission in writing from the author. The only exception is by a reviewer, who may quote short excerpts in a review.

The statements in this book are of the authors and may not be the views of CZYK Publishing or Greater Than a Tourist.

Cover designed by: Ivana Stamenkovic
Cover Image: https://upload.wikimedia.org/wikipedia/commons/4/44/IMG-20170719-124218-bitola-macedonia.jpg

CZYK Publishing Since 2011.

Greater Than a Tourist
Visit our website at www.GreaterThanaTourist.com

Lock Haven, PA
All rights reserved.
ISBN: 9781798494462

>TOURIST

50 TRAVEL TIPS FROM A LOCAL

BOOK DESCRIPTION

Are you excited about planning your next trip?

Do you want to try something new?

Would you like some guidance from a local?

If you answered yes to any of these questions, then this Greater Than a Tourist book is for you.

Greater Than a Tourist- Bitola, Macedonia by Aleksandar Tashkovski offers the inside scoop on Bitola. Most travel books tell you how to travel like a tourist. Although there is nothing wrong with that, as part of the Greater Than a Tourist series, this book will give you travel tips from someone who has lived at your next travel destination.

In these pages, you will discover advice that will help you throughout your stay. This book will not tell you exact addresses or store hours but instead will give you excitement and knowledge from a local that you may not find in other smaller print travel books.

Travel like a local. Slow down, stay in one place, and get to know the people and the culture. By the time you finish this book, you will be eager and prepared to travel to your next destination.

Inside this travel guide book you will find:

- Insider tips from a local.

- Bonus Tips: *50 Things to Know About Packing Light for Travel* by bestselling author Manidipa Bhattacharyya.

- Packing and planning list.

- List of travel questions to ask yourself or others while traveling.

- A place to write your travel bucket list.

OUR STORY

Traveling is a passion of the "Greater than a Tourist" series creator. Lisa studied abroad in college, and for their honeymoon Lisa and her husband toured Europe. During her travels to Malta, an older man tried to give her some advice based on his own experience living on the island since he was a young boy. She was not sure if she should talk to the stranger but was interested in his advice. When traveling to some places she was wary to talk to locals because she was afraid that they weren't being genuine. Through her travels, Lisa learned how much locals had to share with tourists. Lisa created the *Greater Than a Tourist* book series to help connect people with locals. A topic that locals are very passionate about sharing.

TABLE OF CONTENTS

BOOK DESCRIPTION
Our Story
TABLE OF CONTENTS
DEDICATION
ABOUT THE AUTHOR
HOW TO USE THIS BOOK
FROM THE PUBLISHER
WELCOME TO
> TOURIST
1. Baba Mountain
2. River Dragor
3. Consular center
4. Religious and spiritual center
5. The city of pianos and claviers
6. UNESCO Creative cities network
7. Heraclea Lynchestis
8. Bitola plate
9. Sirok sokak
10. Clock tower
11. Warehouse
12. Bitola fortress
13. Deboj amam (public bath)
14. Stara charshija
15. Bezisten

16. Zandan Kule
17. House of Army
18. Military cemeteries and memorials
19. Platanus orientalis
20. Tumbe kafe
21. ZOO garden
22. University Library
23. Filmland
24. Theatre
25. National center for culture
26. Private museum Wagner- Lala
27. Institute and Museum Bitola
28. Museum of Albanian alphabet
29. Private auto- etno museum
30. Memorial museum of Goce Delchev
31. Memorial museum Smilevo
32. Memorial house of Stiv Naumov
33. Manaki Film Festival
34. International festival of folk songs and dances
35. International Monodrama Festival
36. International Summer Festival BIT
37. Bitola Shakespeare Festival
38. Small Montmartre of Bitola
39. International festival of classical music
NTERFEST

>TOURIST

40. International Festival of amateur documentary film CAMERA 300 Bitola
41. International Museum Day
42. Solstis
43. International children music festivals
44. EU and Macedonian Refugee Day
45. Bitola open city
46. Festival of world music
47. Rural tourism
48. Mountain biking, skiing and hiking
49. Celebrities
50. Accomodation, food, night life, transportation

TOP REASONS TO BOOK THIS TRIP
TOP REASONS TO BOOK THIS TRIP
50 THINGS TO KNOW ABOUT PACKING LIGHT FOR TRAVEL
Packing and Planning Tips
Travel Questions
Travel Bucket List
NOTES

>TOURIST

DEDICATION

This book is dedicated to all my fellow citizens, especially to my parents who brought me to life in this beautiful city.

ABOUT THE AUTHOR

Aleksandar Tashkovski is the first Space Law jurist from Bitola, who earned his bachelor's degree in Law at the Ss. Cyril and Methodius University in Skopje where he is finishing his Latin Legum Master's degree in International Law and Relations and Law of the European Union.

Aleksandar is a local from Bitola who will guide you through the tips from his personal experience from the many events throughout the years that are performed in this prosperous cultural, spiritual, historical, economical and scientific center- the city of Bitola.

>TOURIST

HOW TO USE THIS BOOK

The *Greater Than a Tourist* book series was written by someone who has lived in an area for over three months. The goal of this book is to help travelers either dream or experience different locations by providing opinions from a local. The author has made suggestions based on their own experiences. Please do your own research before traveling to the area in case the suggested places are unavailable.

Travel Advisories: As a first step in planning any trip abroad, check the Travel Advisories for your intended destination.
https://travel.state.gov/content/travel/en/traveladvisories/traveladvisories.html

>TOURIST

FROM THE PUBLISHER

Traveling can be one of the most important parts of a person's life. The anticipation and memories that you have are some of the best. As a publisher of the Greater Than a Tourist book series, as well as the popular *50 Things to Know* book series, we strive to help you learn about new places, spark your imagination, and inspire you. Wherever you are and whatever you do I wish you safe, fun, and inspiring travel.

Lisa Rusczyk Ed. D.
CZYK Publishing

>TOURIST

WELCOME TO
> TOURIST

INTRODUCTION

"I'm in love with cities I've never been to and people I've never met."

– John Green.

There is a saying among Macedonians that any intentional or casual traveler that has come in this country, wants to stay a little bit more, come back or move here forever. Macedonia is a rich source of folk art, unrepeatable carving techniques; simply a zenith of world art.

Apart of the other tourist destination like the Ohrid, Prespa or Dojran Lake; the National parks of Mavrovo and Galichica; the Matka Canyon, many beautiful mountains also known internationally and recognized because of their own specific environmental, historical or cultural characteristics; the city of Bitola is one of the most visited cities from tourists in Macedonia.

The city of Bitola is situated sixteen kilometers from Baba Mountain, it is one of the most written about city, second by territory, third by population in the

Republic of Macedonia and was built in the VII century a.c.

In its fourteen centuries history, the city has seen and suffered a lot at the same time, especially with the robberies from the crusade and all those who came against the will of the population assimilating and showing themselves as rulers- Byzantine, Turkish, Serbian, Bulgarian and others.

During its existence the city of Bitola had many other names: Manastiri (during the Ottoman empire, because of the many monasteries in the city) or Obitel (which is an old-Slavic name for a brotherhood of monks). Deciding in accordance with the Bitola plate from 1015 the oldest name of the city is Bitola.

Today, Bitola continues to function as a cultural, historical, consular, economical and scientific center in the south west part of the Republic. With its rich programs, archeological, historical and cultural heritage it attracts many national and international tourists.

It is true that this city doesn't have pyramids, sea, big and exotic beaches, but when you enter the city you can smell the breath of time while witnessing mankind evolution through time immemorial.

All periods have left its own mark in Bitola, marks that are without doubt full of never-ending inspiration for generations and can be found today.

1. BABA MOUNTAIN

The third highest mountain in Macedonia is Baba Mountain (Macedonian: Баба Планина/Baba Planina), also known by the name of its highest peak, Pelister (2601, meters, or 8533 feet). Baba massif splits up the rivers in the region, so that they flow towards the Adriatic. Because of the rich flora and fauna, parts of the Mountain are legally protected as a National Park.

Pelister National Park's flora include the five-needle pine molika (Pinus peuce) - a unique species of tertiary age being present on only a few mountains in the Balkan Peninsula. Fauna in the area include bears, roe deer, Balkan lynx, wolves, chamois, deer, wild boars, rabbits, several species of eagles, partridges, redbilled jackdaws, and the endemic Macedonian Pelagonia trout.

Pelister is the oldest and second largest national park in Macedonia after Mavrovo. It is one of the leading tourist areas in the country, since it is a well-known ski resort, along with Ohrid, Prespa, Dojran, Popova Šapka, and Kruševo.

Pelister provides views of the Pelagonia valley, Lake Prespa, Nidže, Galičica, Jakupica, and the city of Bitola. Pelister is also one of the most southern mountains in the Balkans that has an alpine character. Pelister is also known for its two mountain lakes, which are called Pelister's Eyes, or the Big (2.218 meters) and Small lake (2.180 meters).

2. RIVER DRAGOR

The river Dragor (Macedonian: Драгор) is a small river (25 km) situated in the south of the Republic of Macedonia. It flows mainly through the city of Bitola.

Its spring is in Sapunčica, Lak Potok, Crvena Reka and Klisurnica on the Baba Mountain. The river moves through the village of Dihovo, Bratindol and Pelagonija. The Dragor progression goes to the Aegan Sea through Crna and Vardar river. Because of a flood in 1962 the river is controlled from the fake Strezevo lake.

The river bridges have historical meaning for the city (it has been on Ottoman postcards), especially those built during the Ottoman empire. A project for their reconstruction has been initiated.

3. CONSULAR CENTER

During the Ottoman Empire, Bitola or Monastiri was the capital of the Rumelia Eyalet where all

Consular offices for the Ottoman Empire were settled. During this time there have been twenty consulates while today there are ten honorary consulates and two general consulates showing that the city still has the epithet of Consular City.

Having many consulates in the city means stable economy and wellbeing of locals. Bitolchani (as are the locals called) have had the opportunity to live in a consular center for more than centuries. The geostrategic position of the city, being close to the Aegan and Ionin Sea with a look over Prespa Lake is the reason why this city has been of crucial interest of everyone since ancient times.

The city has fraternizated with Epinal (France), Viena-Center (Austria), Bursa (Turkey), Kremenechuk (Ukraina), Pushkin and Nizhni Novgorod (Russia), Treleborg (Sweden), Rockdale, New South Vales (Australia), Pleven and VelikoTrnovo (Bulgaria), Pozharevac and Stari Grad-Beograd (Serbia), Kranj (Slovenia), Herzeg Novi (Montenegro), Rijeka (Croatia), Ningbo (China). Additionally, a cooperation with the city of Izmir (Turkey), Gorica (Albania), Solun, Kozhani and Voden (Greece) and Kaizerslautern (Germany) have been established.

4. RELIGIOUS AND SPIRITUAL CENTER

There is a reason why Bitola's name during the Ottoman Empire was Monastiri, and the old Slavic meaning of the name Obitel is a monk's brotherhood.

Calculating the different religious centers in the city it can be noticed without doubt the evidence of spirituality in the city. It is believed that there were 40 monasteries during the Ottoman era, while today there are 51 churches and monasteries.

You may still ask yourself why a spiritual and religious center? Well that is because of the coexistence of different religious beliefs in this city. Like that in the center the church of St. Dimitrij (built in 1880), together with the church of St. Bogorodica, St. Sunday and the monastery of Krkrdash are built.

Also, many mosques have been built in the city during the period of the Ottoman Empire. Like that, today there are more mosques that are restored and reopened for believers. One of the most popular mosques are Isak mosque and the Yeni mosque that is in the city center and now is restored and made into a central city artistic gallery.

The Jewish community is represented not only with the cultural protected Jewish cemeteries, the permanent museum setting of the Jewish ethos, but also with the Memorial plaque that is placed on one of the foundations of the Kahal Portugal synagogue in Bitola (central city park).

5. THE CITY OF PIANOS AND CLAVIERS

After the liberation in 1945 in Bitola there were 1200 claviers and pianos. At one point during 1924, in the city there were more pianos and claviers than city lights.

As it is noticed from prof. Ilija Milchin during the biggest economic crisis in the city when people were starving, they refused to sell their pianos and claviers.

This high level of cultural awareness proves without any doubt the always present artistic spirit in Bitola from time immemorial. That is why one of the other nicknames of the city is the city of pianos and claviers.

6. UNESCO CREATIVE CITIES NETWORK

Thanks to Bitola's historical and cultural heritage; respect for film and theatre; the legacy of Manaki Brothers, there are many manifestations throughout the year with creative element which is why this city is on the list of UNESCO Creative cities network.

The Creative cities are focused on promoting sustainable development focused on people and the respect of human rights including its 17 goals to 'make cities and human settlements inclusive, safe, resilient and sustainable' while identifying culture and creativity as one of the essential levers for action in this context.

It is first and foremost at local level that culture and creativity are lived and practiced daily and in Bitola there isn't a day that has passed without any cultural or creative activity organized publicly.

In this regard, UNESCO's Creative Cities Network offers opportunities for cities to draw on peer learning processes and collaborative projects in order to fully capitalize on their creative assets and use this as a basis for building sustainable, inclusive and balanced development in economic, cultural, environmental and social terms.

7. HERACLEA LYNCHESTIS

A town from ancient Macedonian time, built by the Macedonian King Philip II in IV century b.c. represents a heritage in the world open for the public. The name of the city was given from Heracle a mythical hero and founder of the Macedonian royal dynasty, or to be more precise the House of Argeads. The second name Lynchestis comes from the name of this region from that time- Lynchestida and the name of the Macedonian tribe- Lyncestidi.

Heraclea survived many centuries and turbulences, but its heyday as a city was reached during the period of the Roman Empire, more specifically with the construction of Via Ignatia road. With this road the city was connected with Durres and Bosphorus and it was connected diagonally with Stobi and Serdika.

The first excavations were executed in accordance with the special permits issued from the Ottoman Sultan who gave rights to the diplomats for excavation, and the right to buy, or simply take the findings to their own country. This practice stopped with the liberation in 1945, while from 1975 the Institute and Museum Bitola takes care for the place and regardless the massive excavations and movement of the world heritage from Heracle today there are still exponents under the open sky. No doubts why Heraclea Lynchestis has the epithet of the treasure of the Balkans.

Today, this ancient city is restored and put in function. It holds 4 hectares of land, which 1 300 m2 are mosaics; a portico of a courtroom (Roman times), thermal bath (Roman times), theatre (Roman times), Episcopal Residence (Early-Christian period), Small and Great Basilica (Early-Christian period), City fountain (Justinian time).

Many cultural events and happenings are organized in this antique city that is 2 km away from Bitola. Heraclea Lynchestis is one of the rare museums under open skies where you can turn on your travel machine and travel through time.

8. BITOLA PLATE

The so-called Bitola inscription or Bitola plate was founded in 1956 in the Caush mosque and today it is open for the public and can be found in the Bitola Museum.

The plate has a Cyrillic inscription in old Slavic language. The text is about the royal rulers from the Samoil Kingdom who have written about their glory and point of view in history about a heroic battle that was held nearby declaring that the time of the world began from their ruling.

Most researchers are linking this inscription with Tsar Jovan Vladislav, son of Aron (brother of Tsar Samoil), who ruled with the Samoil Kingdom in the period of 1015-1018.

9. SIROK SOKAK

This is the main street of the City protected as a cultural heritage. The main public and intensive cultural life are going on continuously on this street. Its architecture is thanks to the Macedonian constructors who have build a mixture of European and home traditions.

On this street, or Sokak many locals have welcomed many kings and tsars, sultans and vizirs, archbishops and missioners, always feeling the crossroad of East and West. Sirok Sokak represents a common heritage of the world and mankind, having the synonym as one of the most remarkable cultural memorials in the city.

Today, this street is legally protected and renovated. In the past most of the houses were used as consular offices, some of them remain today. Others are privately owned and most of the local cafes are settled here.

10. CLOCK TOWER

One of the most popular memorials that Bitola is known for is the Clock Tower. Scientific research showed that it was built in 1880 during the same period when the church St. Dimitrij was constructed.

There is a saying among locals that the constructors were using a special technique for building the tower. To be more precise in the period of construction 60. 000 eggs were collected from local village households in order to contribute for the construction. It was believed that eggs will give more strength to the walls of the tower and make it more solid.

The Clock Tower is high 33 meters on square basis with 5,8 meters side. On the top there is a dome that gives a splendid panorama of the city. In different eras when the town was under foreign occupation the ownership of the Clock Tower has been changing. Today it measures the time and sings the popular song Bitola my homeland (Битола мој роден крај).

>TOURIST

11. WAREHOUSE

The warehouse in Bitola was a spot where every merchant that was doing business in Bitola was able to put his stock and present it to the locals.

This is one of the many warehouses built in Bitola that is in good shape. Also, the warehouses were used for merchants to negotiate and set up the prize for their stock.

Today this object is transformed into an artistic gallery or to be more precise in Cultural Center Magaza and is used as a place for many different artistic exhibitions and manifestations.

12. BITOLA FORTRESS

The Bitola Fortress (also named as Џепане, from Turkish Cephane/ Dzepane) represents a monument from first category, protected by the Republic. The literal translation of the Turkish and Macedonian word morphology is munition, or to be more precise place for keeping munition.

It was built in 1876 in a form of a cross with unique carved stone. The object can be found in the former military building. The fortress was built by the constructors from Smilevo by the order of the Turkish valija Kjosa Ahmet Zeki pasha. The Ottoman pasha offered money to the constructors, but they refused by saying it is already overly paid pasha, for holy things we do not charge. The pasha figured out when he saw that the fortress is constructed in a form of a cross. After the liberation it was used from the Macedonian military as an arsenal and it was kept as a military secret.

Today, after the closure of the military in Bitola it is open for the public and tourists.

13. DEBOJ AMAM (PUBLIC BATH)

In order to satisfy the hygienic needs of the population the Ottoman Empire was building public baths during its time of rule. There is historic evidence that there have been more than one public baths (some stating that there were even more than ten), but only one is fully restored and conserved and that is the Amam Deboj (Macedonian: Амам Дебој).

One part of the Amam deboj is for women, other for men; there is also a fountain, resting room, massage room, depilation room and private rooms for showering.

>TOURIST

Another public bath that is known, but it's not restored is also in the city center, near the Chinar and the Elementary School Gjorgi Sugarev or behind the building of the Pollice Station.

14. STARA CHARSHIJA

In its long history, Bitola is known as a very important economic center in the Balkans and the merchants from this city were known in the East and West.

The Old bazaar (Macedonian: Стара чаршија/ Stara charshija) was and still is the symbol of the economic life. Today it is protected as a cultural heritage where the breath of life, politics and culture is marked. In the XVII century there were more than 900 shops then in the XIX century their number increased to more than two thousand shops.

The old bazaar in Bitola was known in the whole Ottoman Empire, but during the World War I the bazaar survived the most difficult blow, after which the bazar hasn't returned its economic power.

Today the bazaar in Bitola is renovated, conserved and protected. The local economy with smaller number of shops continues to work and gives life to this old economic center.

15. BEZISTEN

Another cultural monument from the Ottoman Empire is the closed market (Macedonian: Безистен/ Bezisten from Turkish: bedesten) placed by the River Dragor and near the Clock Tower. This market is one of the most valuable and protected old objects in the city with established architectural and aesthetic value.

In the past, the Bezisten was used for selling only precious stock, textile, money, gold, cotton, silk and other valuables. It had a total of 86 shops that inspired every traveler.

Today, the Bezisten is renovated and put into function. There aren't 86 shops, but the economic life of the Bezisten is returned and the people can still feel the crossroad of civilizations through this building while conducting their shopping.

16. ZANDAN KULE

This monument, even though build in the XVII century remains untouched. The story of the monument, which is called Zandan Kule (Macedonian: Зандан Куле in literal translation Prison Tower) relates to the private manners of the effendi, dating from the Ottoman Empire era.

The owner of the building was the local mufti from Bitola. He had built this object in his yard for protection or blood revenge to enemies. It can be entered only with auxiliary stairs.

The object has first floor that was used only from the female members of the family. The tower had its own well and groceries room. Under the roof there are specially built windows for shooting in order to protect from the enemy. Also, the object was commonly used for torturing and prisoning Macedonian revolutionist, which is why the people still remember this building as a prison tower.

17. HOUSE OF ARMY

The architectural expression of the building is typical for the period of historicism in European architecture in terms of plan, decoration and composition tables, with the highlighted Oriental elements. The emergence of these elements in Bitola is normal, when it comes to objects built during the period of the Ottoman rule.

Conceptually the object is built as a synthesis of palace and fortress. Elements of the palace are in the concept of space and masses, and the fortress is visible in the elements in monumental space and secondary decorative plastics derived in the form of cannon tubes.

Officer's house was location for Turkish, Serbian, Bulgarian, Yugoslav and Macedonian army. The doors of this House were once open only for generals and officers, but today its open for the public and occasionally is used as a ballroom or theater stage.

18. MILITARY CEMETERIES AND MEMORIALS

From geostrategic point of view, the location of Bitola was the reason why this place has always been in the focus and interest of foreign militaries.

Regardless of the time or the wars that were on these territories, Bitola has never been forgotten and was always visited from the conquerors. The town has witnessed many sufferings and has taken proper care for the future generations to learn from past mistakes.

>TOURIST

Like that, today three different military cemeteries and memorials exist. Serbian military cemeteries from the Balkan Wars and World War I, where 1321 Serbian soldiers are buried. Also, a French military cemetery and memorial with 13. 262 French soldiers who died in the Macedonian front in World War I. The German military cemeteries and memorial are placed on one of the city hills where 3.406 German soldiers from the Macedonian front and World War I rest and are established and open for the public.

19. PLATANUS ORIENTALIS

The Chinar (Macedonian: Чинар/ Old World sycamore or Oriental Plane) is a big forest tree that can grow high up to 40 meters and 3 meters thickness. This tree is old for more than 6 centuries. It can be found in Ohrid, Bitola, Balkans, Asia and Himalayas.

It is believed that the Chinar was brought to Ohrid and planted by Ss. Kliment Ohridski in the X century a.c.

The Chinar in Bitola is in the city center, nearby the public bath, right behind the police building and the elementary school Gjorgi Sugarev. The tree presents a never-ending inspiration for locals throughout the years. It is believed that a woman from the Ottoman female prison has planted the tree 560 years ago.

20. TUMBE KAFE

This area is settled on a hill in the south part of Bitola and is called Tumbe Kafe. This place is of great significance for locals, since this is the common place among them for leisure and recreation.

On this hill there is a beautiful ZOO garden, also a small amphitheater was built along with an open gym for a quick work out. Behind this hill are the military cemeteries and memorials, next to it is the biggest football stadium in the city.

Tumbe kafe is connected with the biggest park or the central city park of Bitola. The park has open tennis courts, open ice-skating ring, small Luna park, sports hall that is generally used for handball, basketball, bowling, table tennis or concerts.

>TOURIST

21. ZOO GARDEN

The Bitola Zoo was founded in 1951 by a group of committed nature enthusiasts living in the city of Bitola, with mission to preserve existing national and international animal and plant biodiversity through display, breeding and conservation. In 2011, Bitola ZOO by consensus of EAZA was assigned the status of "zoo – candidate under reconstruction".

Bitola Zoo is a municipally owned and public operated facility with more than 30 different species and 400 individual animals.

A complete renovation of the entire physical plant and educational program of the zoo is currently going on and the scope of work includes 26 new animal environments, an education center, hiking trails, viewing platforms, children`s park, restaurant, and service zone.

22. UNIVERSITY LIBRARY

The oldest library in Macedonia is established in 1945 in Bitola. At the beginning this library started with only 300 books. Also, it was changing its headquarters often till 1978 when the official building was restored and upgraded.

Today the National Institution- University Library St. Kliment Ohridski is a modern institution with more than 600.000 books aiming to become a full virtual library.

The building is protected as a cultural heritage and is consisted of two blocks that present one whole. Half of the library is for the readers the other half for the library needs.

23. FILMLAND

The Municipality of Bitola opened a Film Office as a one-stop office for filming in Bitola and Macedonia. The office provides assistance with permits, location identification and access and helps you find the accommodations and the professional and personal services you will need while filming.

This office played a huge role in the filming consciousness of the city and its status as a member of UNESCO Creative cities network.

Some of the films that have been filmed in Bitola are: Before the Rain (1994 film), Dust (2001 film), Goodbye, 20th Century! (1998 film), The Great Water (2004 film), Elveda Rumeli (2009 TV series) and others.

24. THEATRE

The first theatre in Bitola was built by the order of the Wali of Bitola Abdul Kerim-pasha. It was being built for a long period of time, starting in 1897 when the foundation was laid, up till 1908/1909, when it was finally finished. The building was used for various performances, such as festivals, variety and circus shows and theatrical plays. The first professional theatre ensemble worked from 1910 to 1912, when the building was destroyed by the fire. After that, the plays were performed at different locations in the city, but the activity of this ensemble was stopped by the warfare at the Macedonian front.

The second phase of the institutional and professional development of the theatrical activity in Bitola dates from 1918 to 1926/1929, when at the site of the ruined and burnt Turkish theatre, a new building was established in 1926. In the period of 1926 to 1929, the theatre functioned as an organizational part of the Skopje theatre until it ended. Until the beginning of World War II in Bitola there was a rich theater competition because of the many theater groups who played in Serbian language while the Serbian theater in Skopje was always being present with its own repertory in Bitola.

During the World War II and the Nazi occupation, in Bitola the Bulgarian theater was playing, while the alternative stage had few independent groups. Right after the liberation of Bitola a rich theatrical intervention happened, and the first Macedonian professional theater began to play in 14 November 1944.

In November 2013 the theater had 526 premiers, 11.899 shows and more than 5 million visitors.

In addition to the theatrical tradition in the city there is also a long tradition of the independent art stage, which includes more independent amateur theater groups and one hotel-theater that keeps the life of the alternative stage of the city.

25. NATIONAL CENTER FOR CULTURE

The National center for culture was built on the grounds of the former National Theater. Today, this institution hosts a cinema with 3D projections, a small film projection hall and the national theater.

The National center for culture is a place where many of the cultural events and UNESCO festivals are organized and performed. Apart from the cinema in this center, there is also one that is being constructed as a memorial house of the Manaki Brothers and one that is now closed.

26. PRIVATE MUSEUM WAGNER- LALA

The first privately owned museum is the one of Wagner-Lala. Petar Petrov a lawyer and translator opened the museum in honor of Richard Wagner, since Wagner himself has stayed in this house (now a private museum) were also at one-point Franz List was staying.

One of the exponents is a violin that is 181 years old, on which Vagner was teaching the young local Dimtrie Lala, who became his kapellmeister in Wagner's opera.

The violin is made in Austria, has no price and is not on sale.

27. INSTITUTE AND MUSEUM BITOLA

Because of the big amount of cultural and historical world and national heritage on the territory of Bitola, the Ministry for Culture has created an Institute for preservation of monuments of culture and Museum Bitola, or in short Institute and Museum Bitola. In fact, all the tips in this book are under protection and jurisdiction of this institution.

Of course, there are more protected cultural monuments in Bitola than these included in the tips, but It is interesting to notice that the same building of the Institute and Museum is the Military building or to be more precise the Military Academy of Mustafa Kemal Ataturk.

In this massive building that was built to use as a building for the Military Academy of the Ottoman Empire today the Bitola Museum is settled. The same is open for the public and has three permanent museum artefacts: the room of Mustafa Kemal Ataturk, City room interior and the Jewish ethnos.

>TOURIST

28. MUSEUM OF ALBANIAN ALPHABET

In one of the houses in the strong center of the city in the neighborhood that had only royal Ottoman blood the birth of the Albanian alphabet has raised.

In 1900 the Bitola Congress was held by Albanian intellectuals who recognized the need for Albanian alphabet that will be like the European alphabet.

Today the museum is open for the public and the house is reconstructed. There are more than 56 pictures, 230 documents in digital and hard copy with candle figure on display of the intellectuals from the Congress.

29. PRIVATE AUTO- ETNO MUSEUM

Another privately owned museum in Bitola is the Auto and Etno Museum "Filip" in Krklino. Krklino is a village that is 5 kilometers away from Bitola.

The Antique Museum "Filip" contains large collection of antique cars including: Simca Ariane from 1953, Opel Olympia, Ford Taunus, Peugot 404, Plymouth Valiant, Moskvic, Zastava 750, Volkswagen Beetel, Citroen, 24 motorbikes six decades old in a great condition such as BMW, DKW, NSU, MAKS etc.

The museum also has an accommodation and opportunities for rural tourism.

30. MEMORIAL MUSEUM OF GOCE DELCHEV

The memorial museum dedicated to the Macedonian revolutionary Goce Delcev is located in the house, which he made a visit to in Bitola in 1901; this house today is reconstructed as a memorial museum. The main purpose of his visit was to meet his friend and collaborator Dame Gruev, who was at that time in the Bitola Central jail.

In 1977/78, following the complete reconstruction of the building and the preparatory survey, an opening celebration was organized on the occasion of the 85th anniversary of the murder of Goce Delcev on 4 May 1988. The exhibition consists of two halls, which cover an area of 37m2 of which the first hall houses items are connected to the life and the revolutionary activity of this apostle of the Macedonian Liberation movement.

As a continuum of Delchev's revolutionary activity there is a presentation of numerous items presenting the Bitola Revolutionary District. Among the numerous exhibited items of this presentation, you can also see an original item, dating from 1905, embroidery of tiny different colored pearls showing a little deer drinking water, which was given as a gift to Mihail Rakidziev by the prisoners who were together with him in jail.

31. MEMORIAL MUSEUM SMILEVO

On the anniversary of 100 years of the Ilinden Uprising, a decision from the Macedonian government was brought for opening a Memorial Museum in the village of Smilevo.

Covering an area of 130 m2, a museum exhibition was set up, consisting of the following thematic entities: Memorial hall of the Smilevo Congress 1903, Smilevo in the Ilinden Uprising, Memorial hall of the life and revolutionary deeds of Dame Gruev, Memorial hall of the Partisan detachment Dame Gruev, Ethnology hall about Smilevo.

In the Congress hall there is a text, which acquaints the visitor with the contents and the significance of Smilevo, as well as exhibits of more than 27 photos of the members of the Congress and detachments. All presented items are from Smilevo.

32. MEMORIAL HOUSE OF STIV NAUMOV

The house where the national hero Stevan Naumov – Stiv was born is located in the city center or to be more precise on the street Peco Bozinovski No. 11, Bitola.

Among the first activities of the Bitola Museum, actually on the 4th of July 1961, on the Day of the Soldier, there was a promotion of this permanent exhibition, after the reconstruction and adaptation of the building.

In 1977 the building was reconstructed and readapted, thus enabling the conditions for the presentation of the life and acts of Stevan Naumov Stiv. The exhibition is accommodated on an area of more than 150 m2 on the groundfloor and the first floor.

In 2003, this exhibition was renewed for the third time and enriched by new museum items, furthermore on the groundfloor there is an exhibition of the household items and everyday items of the family. On the upper storey of the building, which covers an area of 80 m2 in four separate entities are presented: the documents and items which accompanied the life and work of the hero since his earliest childhood (photos, documents items closely related to his family); while the second entity presents his revolutionary deeds, his death on 12 September 1942 together with his comrade Mite Bogoevski.The history part ends with the presentation of the victory over fascism, and articles written about him.

33. MANAKI FILM FESTIVAL

The Manaki brothers, are Macedonian Vlachs that were born in Rumelia, photography and cinema pioneers of the Balkan Peninsula and the Ottoman Empire. They were the first to bring a film camera and create a motion picture in the city of Bitola (then: Manastir). Their first film, The Weavers, was a 60-second documentary of their grandmother spinning and weaving; this is regarded as the first motion picture shot in the Balkans. The Manaki brothers used a 35 mm Urban Bioscope (under serial number 300) camera that Yanaki imported from London in 1905. Yanaki and Milton filmed documentaries about various aspects of life in the city of Bitola.

Undoubtedly their moving pictures transcended the Balkan film history, while the International Film Festival was born in 1979 thanks to group of film enthusiast.

The International Cinematographers' Film Festival "MANAKI BROTHERS", is the first and oldest film festival dedicated to the creativity of cinematographers across the world.

The festival grew with great potential so that after the Declaration of Independence of the Republic of Macedonia, on the 8th of September, 1991 it was transformed into International Festival of world cinemas represented with feature films, competing for the three festival awards: the Golden, Silver and Bronze Camera 300. Thus Bitola became the Mecca of the best international cinematographers.

\>TOURIST

34. INTERNATIONAL FESTIVAL OF FOLK SONGS AND DANCES

Ilinden Days (Macedonian: Илинденски денови) is an International Festival of Folk songs and Dances that takes place in Bitola every year from 27th July – 2nd August.

This festival is the oldest folk festival in Macedonia and was established in 1971 year supported by the Assembly of the Republic, today from the National Cultural Center of Bitola. This year it will be the 42nd edition of the festival.

The main point of this festival is to cherish the original folklore through research, valuation and presentation of indigenous, original content, expressed in the rich folk cultural treasure and their transfer to future generations as an invaluable cultural value.

35. INTERNATIONAL MONODRAMA FESTIVAL

This festival is also recognized from the UNESCO Creative cities network and it celebrates the stage art through one of the biggest actors' challenges- the monodrama.

The festival is held in May and is recognized by its international component and one of the oldest of this kind in the region.

This festival has a tradition of 20 years, while last year 8 monodramas from Macedonia, USA, Azerbeijan, Poland, Bulgaria, Bosnia and Herzegovina, Russia and Croatia were performing for the Gran Pri reward.

36. INTERNATIONAL SUMMER FESTIVAL BIT

Bit Fest or Bitola Summer Festival is one of the recognized UNESCO events that involves many renowned artists from Macedonia and abroad, and it is held every summer in Bitola.

It is held from June to August and in it are incorporated some other festivals mentioned in this book (like Ilinden and Shakespeare Festival). This festival enriches the cultural offer in Bitola, trough various musical-stage events like theatre, ballet, opera, classical music concerts, art exhibitions, various performances, rock, pop, jazz concerts, etc.

>TOURIST

With a reputation as a city of culture, Bitola through the summer is a locus of many renowned domestic and international artisans. Every day during the summer people from Macedonia and other countries have a chance to fulfill their free time by enjoying what Bitola has to offer.

37. BITOLA SHAKESPEARE FESTIVAL

The idea of organizing the Bitola Shakespeare Festival was born in London 2012 while the theatre was participating in Globe to Globe Festival with our performance „Henry the VI – part three" that was considered very successful. The National Theatre Bitola was one of the few theatres from the Balkans that took part in this grandiose theatre meeting dedicated to Shakespeare.

Bitola Shakespeare Festival is a project of the National Theatre Bitola and it takes place on several stages in the theatre as well as in outdoor open spaces, like the Ancient Theatre of Heraclea.

The interest for the Festival grows every year and the participation in European Network of Shakespeare

Festivals has brought us international companies and worldwide famous directors and theatre workers.

38. SMALL MONTMARTRE OF BITOLA

The former Republic Committee of Culture and Education on the 6th of October 1981 initiated the establishment of the Children Art Studio St. Cyril and Methody- Bitola. The goal of the Studio is gathering young art talents of Bitola's elementary schools and kindergarten facilities. The membership is free of charge, the entry is by competition that is announced at the beginning of the school year.

Children art studio Bitola possess a huge fund of children art works, which now counts more than 400 000 works created by talents from around the world. In aim to present a part of this huge legacy to devotees on fine art the studio organized three huge Guinness exhibitions.

Although this work is still not mentioned in Guinness Book, the studio has opened its first Guinness exhibition at the end of 1995 in the Institute and Museum Bitola. This exhibition consisted of 11058 works selected by international expert jury of the small Montmartre of Bitola. This exhibition was opened for two months and drew a great attention. The exhibition was 1500 kilograms heavy and 800 meters long. The next 1996 second Guinness exhibition was promoted by the Studio. The exhibition was accommodated in the city Museum of Skopje. This exhibition was consisted of 10 000 works.

The third Guinness exhibition organized by the studio was promoted in Belgrade (Serbia) in 1997. The exhibition was accommodated in the Museum of Applied Arts with 3500 works. The studio every year organizes an International Art Colony The Small Montmartre of Bitola were children from all around the world gather together in Bitola to draw.

39. INTERNATIONAL FESTIVAL OF CLASSICAL MUSIC INTERFEST

The international festival of classical music Interfest – Bitola, which is traditionally held from 2nd to 12th October, dates back from 1992.

The festival has national significance, while its program lasts for eleven days and is consisted of 13 - 15 concerts and musical stage performances (opera, ballet), 2 – 3 theater plays and one night of poetry, where eminent Macedonian poets are presented.

The participating ensembles range from solo performers, through chamber orchestras, to symphonic orchestras and choirs. National Theater Bitola is participating every year with premiere play. A significant number of concerts and ballet plays were broadcasted live or recorded by the Macedonian Radio and Television.

Some subsidiary activities at the festival include Master Musical Schools, painting and archeological exhibitions. The Master classes, which are run by remarkable artists – professors of the most distinguished world conservatories, instruct in various practices, such as piano, violin, violoncello, solo singing, trombone, trumpet, clarinet, guitar, etc. In the recent years the Master classes were of a regional character and besides the pupils, students and young artists from Macedonia, candidates from other Eastern European countries also took part.

In the last 18 productions of the festival, over 300 festival events have been performed, presenting artists from fifty countries from Europe, Asia, North and South America, Africa and Australia, many of which are from the leading world music scene.

>TOURIST

40. INTERNATIONAL FESTIVAL OF AMATEUR DOCUMENTARY FILM CAMERA 300 BITOLA

Apart from the International Manaki Film Festival, another International Festival in honor of the camera 300 of Manaki brothers is organized in Bitola; that is the Camera 300- International Festival of amateur documentary film which is held annually in Bitola.

In the past 20 years many films from France, Italy, Russia, Hungary, Austria, Denmark, Serbia, Croatia, Slovenia, Greece, Bulgaria, the USA, Bosnia and Herzegovina, Norway, Moldova, Austria, Turkey, The Czech Republic, The Slovak Republic, Ukraine, Belorussia, England, Israel, Estonia, and of course Macedonia have been awarded.

The standard, caliber and status of the past 20 film editions is recognized by many international jury members who are well-known professionals at this field. Therefore, Camera 300 has a prominent place in the world's non-professional film presentation which is proved by the number of selected films as well as the number of film makers at each festival.

41. INTERNATIONAL MUSEUM DAY

Because of the big number of private and public museums that are open in Bitola, the international day of museums is traditionally celebrated since 1977 in May. The International day of museums is set up by the International Council of Museums with the objective of raising awareness of the fact that, "Museums are an important means of cultural exchange, enrichment of cultures and development of mutual understanding, cooperation and peace among peoples."

The International Museum Council has been accepted from 90 countries. Museums from these countries have an open free-entry day for public and visitors on 18 of May and the same is practiced in Bitola.

The International Council of Museums is an international organisation of museums and museum professionals which is committed to the research, conservation, continuation and communication to society of the world's natural and cultural heritage, present and future, tangible and intangible.

>TOURIST

42. SOLSTIS

In cooperation with the French Republic every year what is known as a holiday of music- Solstis is held in Bitola.

This festival comes as a result of a very close relation between Macedonia and France. Therefore, the Francophonie tradition is respected in Bitola.

On this day, locals get together on the Sirok Sorak and enjoy in ten different improvised stages where music groups, choirs, foreign and home artists from different genres are performing.

43. INTERNATIONAL CHILDREN MUSIC FESTIVALS

In the city of Bitola two international children music festivals are held with a very long tradition.

One of them is TRA LA LA, that is held between 25 states and the other festival is SI DO, which is part of many international organizations where it promotes the Macedonian children's music/song.

Many of today's famous Macedonian singers have been singing and have took part in these international children music festivals.

44. EU AND MACEDONIAN REFUGEE DAY

Every year traditionally the city of Bitola celebrates the EU Day on 8th of May and the Meetings of the survived Macedonian refugees from the Macedonian genocide in Aegean Macedonia.

For the EU day, there is a big happening on the city square were each member of the Union is presented together with the tradition, food, music and symbols of the Union.

Additionally, on 2nd of August the traditional meeting of the survived Macedonian refugees is held in the village of Trnovo in the yard of the church Dormition of Mother of God. The meetings present the unity of Macedonian refugees together with traditional folk dances, songs and food.

45. BITOLA OPEN CITY

The goal of the Festival Bitola Open City (Macedonian: БОГ/ ВОС) is to affirm the positive values, creative energy and its promotion among young and progressive people from the Balkan.

The festival lasts for four days in June as part of BITFEST. The program includes a lot of street concerts, workshops, performances, video projection, public discussions and big music happening.

This festival creates space for civil activism, promotion of democratic values and intercultural relationship, the same is executed by the Youth Cultural Center- Bitola.

46. FESTIVAL OF WORLD MUSIC

The international music festival with its own concept presents a place where international artists can present their music.

Every month in November the Festival takes place in Bitola with a musical repertory and animation for the public from this region. In that way locals can get acquainted with music and culture from many different countries, lay back with a couple of drinks and enjoy the experience.

The festival has a tradition of 10 years and last year special guests was a Cuban music group Compañía Flamenca Ecos.

47. RURAL TOURISM

Around the city there is a vibrant and diverse village life. The territory of the city includes 69 villages.

Some of the villages are developing and offering rural tourism. One of the villages that has this adventure on their menu is Dihovo.

Restored traditional houses with slow food menu are offering tourists a chance to experience the village life under Pelister.

48. MOUNTAIN BIKING, SKIING AND HIKING

Mount bike track with extreme furious letdown, bumps and jumps and fast curves, unforgettable mixture of high speed, adrenaline flow and skillfulness can be found in Pelister, which is also ideal for organizing mount bike contests and races. Some hotels provide Mount bike track which combines many destinations through the National park Pelister in a round tour.

On the other hand, when it comes to skiing the ski-path "Kopanki" is in the length of 1400 m. It's start is in the1800 m height above the sea, and the end is on

>TOURIST

the 1400 m. The cable railway "Bey tap" – Kopanki is located in the length of 680 m. The start is at 1400 m, and the end station at 1610 m. There is a capacity of 450 persons /h in winter and 900 persons/h in summer.Ski-lift "Kopanki" has the length of 580 m. First station is at 1600 m, and the last station is at 1800 m. Capacity is 1000 persons/h. Ski-lift "Pioner" has the length of 230 m, and the path is 350 m.

Furthermore, hiking is always an option for Baba Mountain and a Mountain lodge on Pelister is accepting mountain enthusiasts, fully equipped for sleeping. Also, when it comes to sports in general the Municipility has issued a list of sport terrains in Bitola, such as those for: moto cross, open swimming pool, handball courts, trim roads, recreational hunting, shooting ranges and the sports hall of schools.

49. CELEBRITIES

Since the city of Bitola possess a big amount of cultural and historical common heritages of mankind, without any doubts we can state that Bitola has an international city character.

Like that, there have been many celebrities that visited or lived in Bitola: Brailsford, Henry Noel (1873-1948 English humanist and publicist), Viole, (1859-1925 French Sister of Mercy of the catholi corder, before and after the Ilinden rebellion, greatly contributed to the victims in Bitola's region), Nektarij of Pelagonija, (XVI century, monk, first printer), Ryder, Lady Sye (1923-2000 missionary), Robev, Konstantin (1818-1900 doctor), Harley, the Lady (1916, missionary and benefactor, after the Ilinden rebellion she started Orphan hostel), Sumljanska Zaharija and Sumljanski Julian (missionaries 1864-1937), Thierry Frémont (French actor), Tardu Flordun (Turkish actor), Richard Sammel (German actor), Torsten Voges (German actor), Rade Šerbedžija (Croatian actor), Miki Manojlović (Serbian actor), Mirjana Karanović (Serbian actor), Michael York (English actor), Charles Dance (English actor), Victoria Abril (Spanish actor), Daryl Hannah (American actress), Catherine Deneuve (French actress), Isabelle Huppert (French actress), Julliette Binoche (French actress), Aleksei Serebryakov (Russian actor) and Bruno Ganz (swiss actor).

Also, there have been many international and national celebrities that were born in Bitola: Vasko Tashkovski (painter), Karolina Gocheva (singer), Igor

Durlovski (opera singer), Dimitar Ilievski- Murato (first Macedonian to climb Monteverest), Goran Stefanovski (drama writer) and many other revolutionaries, intellectuals, politicians, directors, diplomats, professors, doctors and judges.

50. ACCOMODATION, FOOD, NIGHT LIFE, TRANSPORTATION

In Bitola there are more than 63 hotels and hostels, from which some offer their own programs for tourists.

There are also more than 59 restaurants where you can taste local and national food.

The main night life is going on Sirok Sokak were the majority of café's are settled. There are 3-night clubs and furthermore the city has also an alternative stage of the night life.

The local transportation is organized with regular local lines while getting to Bitola can be done in more ways. In Macedonia there are two airports Skopje and Ohrid, from both cities you have organized regular transportation with bus, cars or train (for Skopje).

Also, Bitola is easy to reach from the airport in Thessaloniki (Solun), Greece.

>TOURIST

TOP REASONS TO BOOK THIS TRIP

1. HISTORICAL

Walk through the evolution of mankind history from the beginning of time in the city that is the crossroad of East and West.

2. ADVENTOROUS

Are you ready for adrenalin and extreme sporting? Prepare yourself for the best mountain biking, skiing or hiking.

3. CULTURAL

Watch or take part in the daily creative, artistic and cultural events happening in this city without end from time immemorial.

\>TOURIST

OTHER RESOURCES:

A special thanks to all public institutions that allowed the free share of their web information of mankind heritages located in Bitola:

https://bitola.info/

http://bitola.gov.mk/

https://muzejbitola.mk/en/welcome/

https://en.wikipedia.org/wiki/Bitola

https://www.manaki.com.mk/

http://www.camera300.mk/

http://www.interfest.com.mk/

http://bitfest.mk/

http://www.filmlandbitola.org/

https://en.unesco.org/creative-cities/bitola

https://en.wikipedia.org/wiki/Clock_Tower_(Bitola)

https://en.wikipedia.org/wiki/Dragor_(river)

https://en.wikipedia.org/wiki/Baba_Mountain_(North_Macedonia)

https://en.wikipedia.org/wiki/Heraclea_Lyncestis

https://en.wikipedia.org/wiki/%C5%A0irok_Sokak

https://en.wikipedia.org/wiki/Ishak_%C3%87elebi_Mosque

https://en.wikipedia.org/wiki/New_Mosque,_Bitola

https://en.wikipedia.org/wiki/Turkish_bath

https://en.wikipedia.org/wiki/Yanaki_and_Milton_Manak

https://en.wikipedia.org/wiki/Si-Do

http://www.smallmontmartreofbitola.com/

https://bitola.info/churches-and-monasteries/

Links to travel websites or maps of the area:

https://bitola.info/bitola-map/
https://bitola.info/getting-around-bitola/
http://www.hotelmolika.com.mk/
http://www.hotelepinal.com/
http://park-pelister.com/en/
http://www.muzejkrklino.mk/en/
http://www.panacomp.net/villa-in-dihovo-village-rural-tourism-accommodation/

>TOURIST

BONUS BOOK

50 THINGS TO KNOW ABOUT PACKING LIGHT FOR TRAVEL

PACK THE RIGHT WAY EVERY TIME

AUTHOR: MANIDIPA BHATTACHARYYA

First Published in 2015 by Dr. Lisa Rusczyk. Copyright 2015. All Rights Reserved. No part of this publication may be reproduced, including scanning and photocopying, or distributed in any form or by any means, electronic or mechanical, or stored in a database or retrieval system without prior written permission from the publisher.

Disclaimer: The publisher has put forth an effort in preparing and arranging this book. The information provided herein by the author is provided "as is". Use this information at your own risk. The publisher is not a licensed doctor. Consult your doctor before engaging in any medical activities. The publisher and author disclaim any liabilities for any loss of profit or commercial or personal damages resulting from the information contained in this book.

Edited by Melanie Howthorne

ABOUT THE AUTHOR

Manidipa Bhattacharyya is a creative writer and editor, with an education in English literature and Linguistics. After working in the IT industry for seven long years she decided to call it quits and follow her heart instead. Manidipa has been ghost writing, editing, proof reading and doing secondary research services for many story tellers and article writers for about three years. She stays in Kolkata, India with her husband and a busy two year old. In her own time Manidipa enjoys travelling, photography and writing flash fiction.

Manidipa believes in travelling light and never carries anything that she couldn't haul herself on a trip. However, travelling with her child changed the scenario. She seemed to carry the entire world with her for the baby on the first two trips. But good sense prevailed and she is again working her way to becoming a light traveler, this time with a kid.

INTRODUCTION

*He who would travel happily
must travel light.*

-Antoine de Saint-Exupéry

Travel takes you to different places from seas and mountains to deserts and much more. In your travels you get to interact with different people and their cultures. You will, however, enjoy the sights and interact positively with these new people even more, if you are travelling light.

When you travel light your mind can be free from worry about your belongings. You do not have to spend precious vacation time waiting for your luggage to arrive after a long flight. There is be no chance of your bags going missing and the best part is that you need not pay a fee for checked baggage.

People who have mastered this art of packing light will root for you to take only one carry-on, wherever you go. However, many people can find it really hard to pack light. More so if you are travelling with children. Differentiating between "must have" and "just in case" items is the starting point. There will be ample shopping avenues at your destination which are just waiting to be explored.

This book will show you 'packing' in a new 'light' – pun intended – and help you to embrace light packing practices for all of your future travels.

Off to packing!

DEDICATION

I dedicate this book to all the travel buffs that I know, who have given me great insights into the contents of their backpacks.

THE RIGHT TRAVEL GEAR

1. CHOOSE YOUR TRAVEL GEAR CAREFULLY

While selecting your travel gear, pick items that are light weight, durable and most importantly, easy to carry. There are cases with wheels so you can drag them along – these are usually on the heavy side because of the trolley. Alternatively a backpack that you can carry comfortably on your back, or even a duffel bag that you can carry easily by hand or sling across your body are also great options. Whatever you choose, one thing to keep in mind is that the luggage itself should not weigh a ton, this will give you the flexibility to bring along one extra pair of shoes if you so desire.

2. CARRY THE MINIMUM NUMBER OF BAGS

Selecting light weight luggage is not everything. You need to restrict the number of bags you carry as well. One carry-on size bag is ideal for light travel. Most carriers allow one cabin baggage plus one purse, handbag or camera bag as long as it slides under the seat in front. So technically, you can carry two items of luggage without checking them in.

3. PACK ONE EXTRA BAG

Always pack one extra empty bag along with your essential items. This could be a very light weight duffel bag or even a sturdy tote bag which takes up minimal space. In the event that you end up buying a lot of souvenirs, you already have a handy bag to stuff all that into and do not have to spend time hunting for an appropriate bag.

I'm very strict with my packing and have everything in its right place. I never change a rule. I hardly use anything in the hotel room. I wheel my own wardrobe in and that's it.

Charlie Watts

CLOTHES & ACCESSORIES

4. PLAN AHEAD

Figure out in advance what you plan to do on your trip. That will help you to pick that one dress you need for the occasion. If you are going to attend a wedding then you have to carry formal wear. If not, you can ditch the gown for something lighter that will be comfortable during long walks or on the beach.

5. Wear That Jacket

Remember that wearing items will not add extra luggage for your air travel. So wear that bulky jacket that you plan to carry for your trip. This saves space and can also help keep you warm during the chilly flight.

6. MIX AND MATCH

Carry clothes that can be interchangeably used to reinvent your look. Find one top that goes well with a couple of pairs of pants or skirts. Use tops, shirts and jackets wisely along with other accessories like a scarf or a stole to create a new look.

\>TOURIST

7. CHOOSE YOUR FABRIC WISELY

Stuffing clothes in cramped bags definitely takes its toll which results in wrinkles. It is best to carry wrinkle free, synthetic clothes or merino tops. This will eliminate the need for that small iron you usually bring along.

8. DITCH CLOTHES PACK UNDERWEAR

Pack more underwear and socks. These are the things that will give you a fresh feel even if you do not get a chance to wear fresh clothes. Moreover these are easy to wash and can be dried inside the hotel room itself.

9. CHOOSE DARK OVER LIGHT

While picking your clothes choose dark coloured ones. They are easy to colour coordinate and can last longer before needing a wash. Accidental food spills and dirt from the road are less visible on darker clothes.

10. WEAR YOUR JEANS

Take only one pair of Jeans with you, which you should wear on the flight. Remember to pick a pair that can be worn for sightseeing trips and is equally eloquent for dinner. You can add variety by adding light weight cargoes and chinos.

11. CARRY SMART ACCESSORIES

The right accessory can give you a fresh look even with the same old dress. An intelligent neck-piece, a couple of bright scarves, stoles or a sarong can be used in a number of ways to add variety to your clothing. These light weight beauties can double up as a nursing cover, a light blanket, beach wear, a modesty cover for visiting places of worship, and also makes for an enthralling game of peek-a-boo.

12. LEARN TO FOLD YOUR GARMENTS

Seasoned travellers all swear by rolling their clothes for compact and wrinkle free packing. Bundle packing, where you roll the clothes around a central object as if tying it up, is also a popular method of compact and wrinkle free packing. Stacking folded clothes one on top of another is a big no-no as it makes creases extreme and they are difficult to get rid of without ironing.

>TOURIST

13. WASH YOUR DIRTY LAUNDRY

One of the ways to avoid carrying loads of clothes is to wash the clothes you carry. At some places you might get to use the laundry services or a Laundromat but if you are in a pinch, best solution is to wash them yourself. If that is the plan then carrying quick drying clothes is highly recommended, which most often also happen to be the wrinkle free variety.

14. LEAVE THOSE TOWELS BEHIND

Regular towels take up a lot of space, are heavy and take ages to dry out. If you are staying at hotels they will provide you with towels anyway. If you are travelling to a remote place, where the availability of towels look doubtful, carry a light weight travel towel of viscose material to do the job.

15. USE A COMPRESSION BAG

Compression bags are getting lots of recommendation now days from regular travellers. These are useful for saving space in your luggage when you have to pack bulky dresses. While packing for the return trip, get help from the hotel staff to arrange a vacuum cleaner.

FOOTWEAR

16. PUT ON YOUR HIKING BOOTS

If you have plans to go hiking or trekking during your trip, you will need those bulky hiking boots. The best way to carry them is to wear them on flight to save space and luggage weight. You can remove the boots once inside and be comfortable in your socks.

17. PICKING THE RIGHT SHOES

Shoes are often the bulkiest items, along with being the dainty if you are a female. They need care and take up a lot of space in your luggage. It is advisable therefore to pick shoes very carefully. If you plan to do a lot of walking and site seeing, then wearing a pair of comfortable walking shoes are a must. For more formal occasions you can carry durable, light weight flats which will not take up much space.

18. STUFF SHOES

If you happen to pack a pair of shoes, ensure you utilize their hollow insides. Tuck small items like rolled up socks or belts to save space. They will also be easy to find.

>TOURIST

TOILETRIES

19. STASHING TOILETRIES

Carry only absolute necessities. Airline rules dictate that for one carry-on bag, liquids and gels must be in 3.4 ounce (100ml) bottles or less, and must be packed in a one quart zip-lock bag. If you are planning to stay in a hotel, the basic things will be provided for you. It's best is to buy the rest from the local market at your destination.

20. TAKE ALONG TAMPONS

Tampons are a hard to find item in a lot of countries. Figure out how many you need and pack accordingly. For longer stays you can buy them online and have them delivered to where you are staying.

21. GET PAMPERED BEFORE YOU TRAVEL

Some avid travellers suggest getting a pedicure and manicure just the day before travelling. This not only gives you a well kept look, you also save the trouble of packing nail polish. Remember, every little bit of weight reduced adds up.

ELECTRONICS

22. LUGGING ALONG ELECTRONICS

Electronics have a large role to play in our lives today. Most of us cannot imagine our lives away from our phones, laptops or tablets. However while travelling, one must consider the amount of weight these electronics add to our luggage. Thankfully smart phones come along with all the essentials tools like a camera, email access, picture editing tools and more. They are smart to the point of eliminating the need to carry multiple gadgets. Choose a smart phone that suits all your requirements and travel with the world in your palms or pocket.

23. REDUCE THE NUMBER OF CHARGERS

If you do travel with multiple electronic devices, you will have to bear the additional burden of carrying all their chargers too. Check if a single charger can be used for multiple devices. You might also consider investing in a pocket charger. These small devices support multiple devices while keeping you charged on the go.

>TOURIST

24. TRAVEL FRIENDLY APPS

Along with smart phones come numerous apps, which are immensely helpful in our travels. You name it and you have an app for it at hand – take pictures, sharing with friends and family, torch to light dark roads, maps, checking flight/train times, find hotels and many other things. Use these smart alternatives to traditional items like books to eliminate weight and save space.

I get ideas about what's essential when packing my suitcase.

-Diane von Furstenberg

TRAVELLING WITH KIDS

25. BRING ALONG THE STROLLER

Kids might enjoy walking for a while but they soon tire out and a stroller is the just the right thing for them to rest in while you continue your tour. Strollers also double duty as a luggage carrier and shopping bag holder. Remember to pick a light weight, easy to handle brand of stroller. Better yet, find out in advance if you can rent a stroller at your destination.

26. BRING ONLY ENOUGH DIAPERS FOR YOUR TRIP

Diapers take up a lot of space and add to the weight of your luggage. Therefore it is advisable to carry just enough diapers to last through the trip and a few for afterwards, till you buy fresh stock at your destination. Unless of course you are travelling to a really remote area, in which case you have no choice but to carry the load. Otherwise diapers are something you will find pretty easily.

27. TAKE ONLY A COUPLE OF TOYS

Children are easily attracted by new things in their environment. While travelling they will find numerous 'new' objects to scrutinize and play with. Packing just one favorite toy is enough, or if there is no favorite toy leave out all of them in favor of stories or imaginary games.

28. CARRY KID FRIENDLY SNACKS

Create a small snack counter in your bag to store away quick bites for those sudden hunger pangs. Depending on the child's age this could include chocolates, raisins, dry fruits, granola bars or biscuits.

>TOURIST

Also keep a bottle of water handy for your little one. These things do not add much weight and can be adjusted in a handbag or knapsack.

29. GAMES TO CARRY

Create some travel specific, imaginary games if you have slightly grown up children, like spot the attractions. Keep a coloring book and colors handy for in-flight or hotel time. Apps on your smart phone can keep the children engaged with cartoons and story books. Older children are often entertained by games available on phones or tablets. This cuts the weight of luggage down while keeping the kids entertained.

30. LET THE KIDS CARRY THEIR LOAD

A good thing is to start early sharing of responsibilities. Let your child pick a bag of his or her choice and pack it themselves. Keep tabs on what they are stuffing in their bags by asking if they will be using that item on the trip. It could start out being just an entertainment bag initially but with growing years they will learn to sort the useful from the superfluous. Children as little as four can maneuver a small trolley suitcase like a pro- their experience in pull along toys credit. If you are worried that you may be pulling it for them, you may want to start with a backpack.

31. DECIDE ON LOCATION FOR CHILDREN TO SLEEP

While on a trip you might not always get a crib at your destination, and carrying one will make life all the more difficult. Instead call ahead to see if there are any cribs or roll out beds for children. You may even put blankets on the floor. Weave them a story about camping and they will gladly sleep without any trouble.

32. GET BABY PRODUCTS DELIVERED AT YOUR DESTINATION

If you are absolutely paranoid about not getting your favourite variety of diaper or brand of baby food, check out online stores like amazon.com for services in your destination city. You can buy things online ahead of your travel and get them delivered to your hotel upon arrival.

33. FEEDING NEEDS OF YOUR INFANTS

If you are travelling with a breastfed infant, you save the trouble of carrying bottles and bottle sanitization kits. For special food, or medications, you may need to call ahead to make sure you have a refrigerator where you are staying.

34. FEEDING NEEDS OF YOUR TODDLER

With the progression from infancy to toddler, their dietary requirements too evolve. You will have to pack some snacks for travelling time. Fresh fruits and vegetables can be purchased at your destination. Most of the cities you travel to in whichever part of the world, will have baby food products and formulas, available at the local drug-store or the supermarket.

35. PICKING CLOTHES FOR YOUR BABY

Contrary to popular belief, babies can do without many changes of clothes. At the most pack 2 outfits per day. Pack mix and match type clothes for your little one as well. Pick things which are comfortable to wear and quick to dry.

36. SELECTING SHOES FOR YOUR BABY

Like outfits, kids can make do with two pairs of comfortable shoes. If you can get some water resistant shoes it will be best. To expedite drying wet shoes, you can stuff newspaper in them then wrap them with newspaper and leave them to dry overnight.

37. KEEP ONE CHANGE OF CLOTHES HANDY

Travelling with kids can be tricky. Keep a change of clothes for the kids and mum handy in your purse or tote bag. This takes a bit of space in your hand luggage but comes extremely handy in case there are any accidents or spills.

38. LEAVE BEHIND BABY ACCESSORIES

Baby accessories like their bed, bath tub, car seat, crib etc. should be left at home. Many hotels provide a crib on request, while car seats can be borrowed from friends or rented. Babies can be given a bath in the hotel sink or even in the adult bath tub with a little bit of water. If you bring a few bath toys, they can be used in the bath, pool, and out of water. They can also be sanitized easily in the sink.

39. CARRY A SMALL LOAD OF PLASTIC BAGS

With children around there are chances of a number of soiled clothes and diapers. These plastic bags help to sort the dirt from the clean inside your big bag.

These are very light weight and come in handy to other carry stuff as well at times.

PACK WITH A PURPOSE

40. PACKING FOR BUSINESS TRIPS

One neutral-colored suit should suffice. It can be paired with different shirts, ties and accessories for different occasions. One pair of black suit pants could be worn with a matching jacket for the office or with a snazzy top for dinner.

41. PACKING FOR A CRUISE

Most cruises have formal dinners, and that formal dress usually takes up a lot of space. However you might find a tuxedo to rent. For women, a short black dress with multiple accessory options will do the trick.

42. PACKING FOR A LONG TRIP OVER DIFFERENT CLIMATES

The secret packing mantra for travel over multiple climates is layering. Layering traps air around your body creating insulation against the cold. The same light t-shirt that is comfortable in a warmer climate can be the innermost layer in a colder climate.

REDUCE SOME MORE WEIGHT

43. LEAVE PRECIOUS THINGS AT HOME

Things that you would hate to lose or get damaged leave them at home. Precious jewelry, expensive gadgets or dresses, could be anything. You will not require these on your trip. Leave them at home and spare the load on your mind.

44. SEND SOUVENIRS BY MAIL

If you have spent all your money on purchasing souvenirs, carrying them back in the same bag that you brought along would be difficult. Either pack everything in another bag and check it in the airport or get everything shipped to your home. Use an international carrier for a secure transit, but this could be more expensive than the checking fees at the airport.

45. AVOID CARRYING BOOKS

Books equal to weight. There are many reading apps which you can download on your smart phone or tab.

> TOURIST

Plus there are gadgets like Kindle and Nook that are thinner and lighter alternatives to your regular book.

CHECK, GET, SET, CHECK AGAIN

46. STRATEGIZE BEFORE PACKING

Create a travel list and prepare all that you think you need to carry along. Keep everything on your bed or floor before packing and then think through once again – do I really need that? Any item that meets this question can be avoided. Remove whatever you don't really need and pack the rest.

47. TEST YOUR LUGGAGE

Once you have fully packed for the trip take a test trip with your luggage. Take your bags and go to town for window shopping for an hour. If you enjoy your hour long trip it is good to go, if not, go home and reduce the load some more. Repeat this test till you hit the right weight.

48. ADD A ROLL OF DUCT TAPE

You might wonder why, when this book has been talking about reducing stuff, we're suddenly asking you to pack something totally unusual. This is because when you have limited supplies, duct tape is immensely helpful for small repairs – a broken bag, leaking zip-lock bag, broken sunglasses, you name it and duct tape can fix it, temporarily.

49. LIST OF ESSENTIAL ITEMS

Even though the emphasis is on packing light, there are things which have to be carried for any trip. Here is our list of essentials:

- Passport/Visa or any other ID

- Any other paper work that might be required on a trip like permits, hotel reservation confirmations etc.

- Medicines – all your prescription medicines and emergency kit, especially if you are travelling with children

- Medical or vaccination records

- Money in foreign currency if travelling to a different country

- Tickets- Email or Message them to your phone

\>TOURIST

50. MAKE THE MOST OF YOUR TRIP

Wherever you are going, whatever you hope to do we encourage you to embrace it whole-heartedly. Take in the scenery, the culture and above all, enjoy your time away from home.

On a long journey even a straw weighs heavy.

-Spanish Proverb

>TOURIST

PACKING AND PLANNING TIPS

A Week before Leaving

- Arrange for someone to take care of pets and water plants.
- Stop mail and newspaper.
- Notify Credit Card companies where you are going.
- Change your thermostat settings.
- Car inspected, oil is changed, and tires have the correct pressure.
- Passports and photo identification is up to date.
- Pay bills.
- Copy important items and download travel Apps.
- Start collecting small bills for tips.

Right Before Leaving

- Clean out refrigerator.
- Empty garbage cans.
- Lock windows.
- Make sure you have the proper identification with you.
- Bring cash for tips.
- Remember travel documents.
- Lock door behind you.
- Remember wallet.
- Unplug items in house and pack chargers.

\>TOURIST

READ OTHER GREATER THAN A TOURIST BOOKS

Greater Than a Tourist San Miguel de Allende Guanajuato Mexico: 50 Travel Tips from a Local by Tom Peterson

Greater Than a Tourist – Lake George Area New York USA: 50 Travel Tips from a Local by Janine Hirschklau

Greater Than a Tourist – Monterey California United States: 50 Travel Tips from a Local by Katie Begley

Greater Than a Tourist – Chanai Crete Greece: 50 Travel Tips from a Local by Dimitra Papagrigoraki

Greater Than a Tourist – The Garden Route Western Cape Province South Africa: 50 Travel Tips from a Local by Li-Anne McGregor van Aardt

Greater Than a Tourist – Sevilla Andalusia Spain: 50 Travel Tips from a Local by Gabi Gazon

Greater Than a Tourist – Kota Bharu Kelantan Malaysia: 50 Travel Tips from a Local by Aditi Shukla

Children's Book: Charlie the Cavalier Travels the World by Lisa Rusczyk

> TOURIST

Visit *Greater Than a Tourist* for Free Travel Tips
http://GreaterThanATourist.com

Sign up for the *Greater Than a Tourist* Newsletter for discount days, new books, and travel information:
http://eepurl.com/cxspyf

Follow us on Facebook for tips, images, and ideas:
https://www.facebook.com/GreaterThanATourist

Follow us on Pinterest for travel tips and ideas:
http://pinterest.com/GreaterThanATourist

Follow us on Instagram for beautiful travel images:
http://Instagram.com/GreaterThanATourist

At *Greater Than a Tourist*, we love to share travel tips with you. How did we do? What guidance do you have for how we can give you better advice for your next trip? Please send your feedback to GreaterThanaTourist@gmail.com as we continue to improve the series. We appreciate your constructive feedback. Thank you.

>TOURIST

METRIC CONVERSIONS

TEMPERATURE

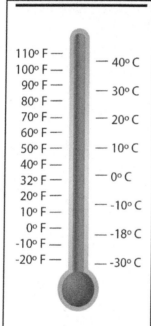

110° F — 40° C
100° F
90° F — 30° C
80° F
70° F — 20° C
60° F
50° F — 10° C
40° F
32° F — 0° C
20° F
10° F — -10° C
0° F
-10° F — -18° C
-20° F — -30° C

To convert F to C:
Subtract 32, and then multiply by 5/9 or .5555.

To Convert C to F:
Multiply by 1.8 and then add 32.

32F = 0C

LIQUID VOLUME

To Convert:	Multiply by
U.S. Gallons to Liters	3.8
U.S. Liters to Gallons	26
Imperial Gallons to U.S. Gallons	1.2
Imperial Gallons to Liters	4.55
Liters to Imperial Gallons	22

1 Liter = .26 U.S. Gallon
1 U.S. Gallon = 3.8 Liters

DISTANCE

To convert	Multiply by
Inches to Centimeters	2.54
Centimeters to Inches	39
Feet to Meters	.3
Meters to Feet	3.28
Yards to Meters	91
Meters to Yards	1.09
Miles to Kilometers	1.61
Kilometers to Miles	.62

1 Mile = 1.6 km
1 km = .62 Miles

WEIGHT

1 Ounce = .28 Grams
1 Pound = .4555 Kilograms
1 Gram = .04 Ounce
1 Kilogram = 2.2 Pounds

>TOURIST

TRAVEL QUESTIONS

- Do you bring presents home to family or friends after a vacation?
- Do you get motion sick?
- Do you have a favorite billboard?
- Do you know what to do if there is a flat tire?
- Do you like a sun roof open?
- Do you like to eat in the car?
- Do you like to wear sun glasses in the car?
- Do you like toppings on your ice cream?
- Do you use public bathrooms?
- Did you bring your cell phone and does it have power?
- Do you have a form of identification with you?
- Have you ever been pulled over by a cop?
- Have you ever given money to a stranger on a road trip?
- Have you ever taken a road trip with animals?
- Have you ever went on a vacation alone?

- Have you ever run out of gas?
- If you could move to any place in the world, where would it be?
- If you could travel anywhere in the world, where would you travel?
- If you could travel in any vehicle, which one would it be?
- If you had three things to wish for from a magic genie, what would they be?
- If you have a driver's license, how many times did it take you to pass the test?
- What are you the most afraid of on vacation?
- What do you want to get away from the most when you are on vacation?
- What foods smells bad to you?
- What item do you bring on ever trip with you away from home?
- What makes you sleepy?
- What song would you love to hear on the radio when you're cruising on the highway?
- What travel job would you want the least?
- What will you miss most while you are away from home?
- What is something you always wanted to try?

>TOURIST

- What is the best road side attraction that you ever saw?
- What is the farthest distance you ever biked?
- What is the farthest distance you ever walked?
- What is the weirdest thing you needed to buy while on vacation?
- What is your favorite candy?
- What is your favorite color car?
- What is your favorite family vacation?
- What is your favorite food?
- What is your favorite gas station drink or food?
- What is your favorite license plate design?
- What is your favorite restaurant?
- What is your favorite smell?
- What is your favorite song?
- What is your favorite sound that nature makes?
- What is your favorite thing to bring home from a vacation?
- What is your favorite vacation with friends?
- What is your favorite way to relax?

- Where is the farthest place you ever traveled in a car?
- Where is the farthest place you ever went North, South, East and West?
- Where is your favorite place in the world?
- Who is your favorite singer?
- Who taught you how to drive?
- Who will you miss the most while you are away?
- Who if the first person you will contact when you get to your destination?
- Who brought you on your first vacation?
- Who likes to travel the most in your life?
- Would you rather be hot or cold?
- Would you rather drive above, below, or at the speed limited?
- Would you rather drive on a highway or a back road?
- Would you rather go on a train or a boat?
- Would you rather go to the beach or the woods?

\>TOURIST

TRAVEL BUCKET LIST

1.

2.

3.

4.

5.

6.

7.

8.

9.

10.

>TOURIST

NOTES

Made in the USA
Monee, IL
09 April 2021

65248976R00069